I0796460

To:
From:
Date:

Christian Art
GIFTS

"Be strong and courageous!
For the LORD your God is with you wherever you go."

JOSH. 1:9

He made us, and we are His. We are His people, the sheep of His pasture.

Ps. 100:3

Give your burdens to the LORD, and He will take care of you.

PS. 55:22

Let God transform you into a new person by changing the way you think.

Rom. 12:2

"God blesses those who work for peace,
for they will be called the children of God."

MATT. 5:9

"Anything is possible if a person believes."

Mark 9:23

I can do everything through Christ, who gives me strength.

PHIL. 4:13

"Blessed are those who trust in the LORD and have made the LORD their hope and confidence."

JER. 17:7

The LORD leads with unfailing love and faithfulness
all who keep His covenant and obey His demands.

Ps. 25:10

"Come to Me, all of you who are weary and carry heavy burdens, and I will give you rest."

MATT. 11:28

"Do not be afraid or discouraged,
for the LORD will personally go ahead of you."

DEUT. 31:8

Those who live in the shelter of the Most High will find rest
in the shadow of the Almighty.

Ps. 91:1

"I will never fail you. I will never abandon you."

HEB. 13:5

Kind words are like honey – sweet to the soul and healthy for the body.

Prov. 16:24

"The joy of the Lord is your strength!"

Neh. 8:10

This is the day the LORD has made.
We will rejoice and be glad in it.

Ps. 118:24

Those who trust in the LORD will find new strength.
They will soar high on wings like eagles.

ISA. 40:31

"No eye has seen, no ear has heard, and no mind has imagined what God has prepared for those who love Him."

1 Cor. 2:9

I will rejoice in the LORD! I will be joyful in the God of my salvation!

HAB. 3:18

Nothing in all creation will ever be able to separate us from the love of God.

Rom. 8:39

My health may fail, and my spirit may grow weak, but God remains the strength of my heart; He is mine forever.

Ps. 73:26

See how very much our Father loves us, for He calls us
His children, and that is what we are!

1 John 3:1

"Blessed are all who hear the word of God
and put it into practice."

Luke 11:28

The LORD is my light and my salvation –
so why should I be afraid?

Ps. 27:1

The LORD is my strength and my song; He has given me victory.
This is my God, and I will praise Him.

EXOD. 15:2

May the Lord of peace Himself give you His peace
at all times and in every situation.

2 Thess. 3:16

Let the peace that comes from Christ rule in your hearts.
For as members of one body you are called to live in peace.

Col. 3:15

Lord my God, I cried to You for help, and You restored my health.

Ps. 30:2

"Those who exalt themselves will be humbled,
and those who humble themselves will be exalted."

MATT. 23:12

"Do not be afraid, for I have ransomed you. I have called you by name; you are Mine. When you go through deep waters, I will be with you."

Isa. 43:1-2

"Be still, and know that I am God!"

Ps. 46:10

"I know the plans I have for you," says the LORD. "They are plans for good and not for disaster, to give you a future and a hope."

JER. 29:11

"Be strong and courageous!
For the LORD your God is with you wherever you go."

JOSH. 1:9

He made us, and we are His. We are His people, the sheep of His pasture.

Ps. 100:3

Give your burdens to the LORD, and He will take care of you.

Ps. 55:22

Let God transform you into a new person by changing the way you think.

Rom. 12:2

"God blesses those who work for peace,
for they will be called the children of God."

Matt. 5:9

"Anything is possible if a person believes."

Mark 9:23

I can do everything through Christ, who gives me strength.

Phil. 4:13

"Blessed are those who trust in the LORD and have made the LORD their hope and confidence."

JER. 17:7

The LORD leads with unfailing love and faithfulness
all who keep His covenant and obey His demands.

Ps. 25:10

"Come to Me, all of you who are weary and carry heavy burdens, and I will give you rest."

Matt. 11:28

"Do not be afraid or discouraged,
for the LORD will personally go ahead of you."

DEUT. 31:8

Those who live in the shelter of the Most High will find rest
in the shadow of the Almighty.

Ps. 91:1

"I will never fail you. I will never abandon you."

HEB. 13:5

Kind words are like honey – sweet to the soul and healthy for the body.

Prov. 16:24

"The joy of the LORD is your strength!"

NEH. 8:10

This is the day the LORD has made.
We will rejoice and be glad in it.

Ps. 118:24

Those who trust in the LORD will find new strength.
They will soar high on wings like eagles.

ISA. 40:31

"No eye has seen, no ear has heard, and no mind has imagined what God has prepared for those who love Him."

1 Cor. 2:9

I will rejoice in the LORD! I will be joyful in the God of my salvation!

HAB. 3:18

Nothing in all creation will ever be able to separate us from the love of God.

Rom. 8:39

My health may fail, and my spirit may grow weak, but God remains the strength of my heart; He is mine forever.

Ps. 73:26

See how very much our Father loves us, for He calls us
His children, and that is what we are!

1 John 3:1

"Blessed are all who hear the word of God
and put it into practice."

Luke 11:28

The LORD is my light and my salvation –
so why should I be afraid?

Ps. 27:1

The LORD is my strength and my song; He has given me victory.
This is my God, and I will praise Him.

EXOD. 15:2

May the Lord of peace Himself give you His peace
at all times and in every situation.

2 Thess. 3:16

Let the peace that comes from Christ rule in your hearts.
For as members of one body you are called to live in peace.

Col. 3:15

LORD my God, I cried to You for help, and You restored my health.

Ps. 30:2

"Those who exalt themselves will be humbled,
and those who humble themselves will be exalted."

Matt. 23:12

"Do not be afraid, for I have ransomed you. I have called you by name; you are Mine. When you go through deep waters, I will be with you."

Isa. 43:1-2

"Be still, and know that I am God!"

Ps. 46:10

"I know the plans I have for you," says the LORD. "They are plans for good and not for disaster, to give you a future and a hope."

JER. 29:11

"Be strong and courageous!
For the LORD your God is with you wherever you go."

JOSH. 1:9

He made us, and we are His. We are His people, the sheep of His pasture.

Ps. 100:3

Give your burdens to the LORD, and He will take care of you.

Ps. 55:22

Let God transform you into a new person by changing the way you think.

Rom. 12:2

"God blesses those who work for peace,
for they will be called the children of God."

Matt. 5:9

"Anything is possible if a person believes."

MARK 9:23

I can do everything through Christ, who gives me strength.

Phil. 4:13

"Blessed are those who trust in the LORD and have made the LORD their hope and confidence."

JER. 17:7

The LORD leads with unfailing love and faithfulness
all who keep His covenant and obey His demands.

Ps. 25:10

"Come to Me, all of you who are weary and carry heavy burdens,
and I will give you rest."

Matt. 11:28

"Do not be afraid or discouraged,
for the LORD will personally go ahead of you."

DEUT. 31:8

Those who live in the shelter of the Most High will find rest
in the shadow of the Almighty.

Ps. 91:1

"I will never fail you. I will never abandon you."

Heb. 13:5

Kind words are like honey – sweet to the soul and healthy for the body.

Prov. 16:24

"The joy of the Lord is your strength!"

Neh. 8:10

This is the day the LORD has made.
We will rejoice and be glad in it.

Ps. 118:24

Those who trust in the LORD will find new strength.
They will soar high on wings like eagles.

ISA. 40:31

"No eye has seen, no ear has heard, and no mind has imagined what God has prepared for those who love Him."

1 Cor. 2:9

I will rejoice in the LORD! I will be joyful in the God of my salvation!

HAB. 3:18

Nothing in all creation will ever be able to separate us from the love of God.

ROM. 8:39

My health may fail, and my spirit may grow weak, but God remains the strength of my heart; He is mine forever.

Ps. 73:26

See how very much our Father loves us, for He calls us
His children, and that is what we are!

1 John 3:1

"Blessed are all who hear the word of God
and put it into practice."

Luke 11:28

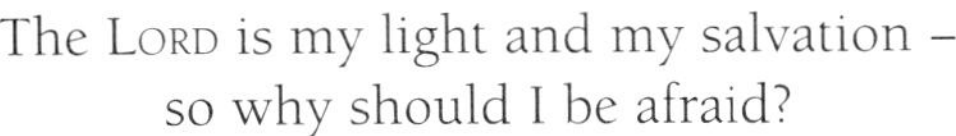

The Lord is my light and my salvation –
so why should I be afraid?

Ps. 27:1

The LORD is my strength and my song; He has given me victory.
This is my God, and I will praise Him.

EXOD. 15:2

May the Lord of peace Himself give you His peace
at all times and in every situation.

2 Thess. 3:16

Let the peace that comes from Christ rule in your hearts.
For as members of one body you are called to live in peace.

Col. 3:15

Lord my God, I cried to You for help, and You restored my health.

Ps. 30:2

"Those who exalt themselves will be humbled,
and those who humble themselves will be exalted."

MATT. 23:12

"Do not be afraid, for I have ransomed you. I have called you by name; you are Mine. When you go through deep waters, I will be with you."

Isa. 43:1-2

"Be still, and know that I am God!"

Ps. 46:10

"I know the plans I have for you," says the LORD. "They are plans for good and not for disaster, to give you a future and a hope."

JER. 29:11

"Be strong and courageous!
For the LORD your God is with you wherever you go."

JOSH. 1:9

He made us, and we are His. We are His people, the sheep of His pasture.

Ps. 100:3

Give your burdens to the LORD, and He will take care of you.

PS. 55:22

Let God transform you into a new person by changing the way you think.

ROM. 12:2

"God blesses those who work for peace,
for they will be called the children of God."

Matt. 5:9

"Anything is possible if a person believes."

MARK 9:23

I can do everything through Christ, who gives me strength.

PHIL. 4:13

"Blessed are those who trust in the LORD and have made the LORD their hope and confidence."

JER. 17:7

The LORD leads with unfailing love and faithfulness
all who keep His covenant and obey His demands.

Ps. 25:10

"Come to Me, all of you who are weary and carry heavy burdens, and I will give you rest."

Matt. 11:28

"Do not be afraid or discouraged,
for the LORD will personally go ahead of you."

DEUT. 31:8

Those who live in the shelter of the Most High will find rest
in the shadow of the Almighty.

Ps. 91:1

"I will never fail you. I will never abandon you."

HEB. 13:5

Kind words are like honey – sweet to the soul and healthy for the body.

Prov. 16:24

"The joy of the LORD is your strength!"

NEH. 8:10

This is the day the LORD has made.
We will rejoice and be glad in it.

Ps. 118:24

Those who trust in the LORD will find new strength.
They will soar high on wings like eagles.

ISA. 40:31

"No eye has seen, no ear has heard, and no mind has imagined what God has prepared for those who love Him."

1 Cor. 2:9

I will rejoice in the LORD! I will be joyful in the God of my salvation!

HAB. 3:18

Nothing in all creation will ever be able to separate us from the love of God.

ROM. 8:39

My health may fail, and my spirit may grow weak, but God remains
the strength of my heart; He is mine forever.

Ps. 73:26

See how very much our Father loves us, for He calls us
His children, and that is what we are!

1 John 3:1

"Blessed are all who hear the word of God
and put it into practice."

Luke 11:28

The Lord is my light and my salvation –
so why should I be afraid?

Ps. 27:1

The LORD is my strength and my song; He has given me victory.
This is my God, and I will praise Him.

EXOD. 15:2

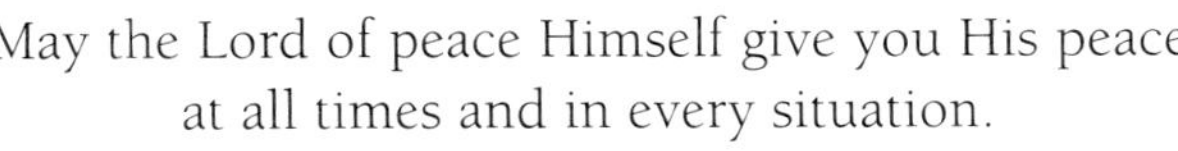

May the Lord of peace Himself give you His peace
at all times and in every situation.

2 Thess. 3:16

Let the peace that comes from Christ rule in your hearts.
For as members of one body you are called to live in peace.

Col. 3:15

LORD my God, I cried to You for help, and You restored my health.

Ps. 30:2

"Those who exalt themselves will be humbled,
and those who humble themselves will be exalted."

MATT. 23:12

"Do not be afraid, for I have ransomed you. I have called you by name; you are Mine. When you go through deep waters, I will be with you."

Isa. 43:1-2

"Be still, and know that I am God!"

Ps. 46:10

"I know the plans I have for you," says the Lord. "They are plans for good and not for disaster, to give you a future and a hope."

Jer. 29:11

"Be strong and courageous!
For the LORD your God is with you wherever you go."

JOSH. 1:9

He made us, and we are His. We are His people, the sheep of His pasture.

Ps. 100:3

Give your burdens to the Lord, and He will take care of you.

Ps. 55:22

Let God transform you into a new person by changing the way you think.

Rom. 12:2

"God blesses those who work for peace,
for they will be called the children of God."

Matt. 5:9

"Anything is possible if a person believes."

Mark 9:23

I can do everything through Christ, who gives me strength.

PHIL. 4:13

"Blessed are those who trust in the LORD and have made the LORD their hope and confidence."

JER. 17:7

The LORD leads with unfailing love and faithfulness
all who keep His covenant and obey His demands.

PS. 25:10

"Come to Me, all of you who are weary and carry heavy burdens, and I will give you rest."

MATT. 11:28

"Do not be afraid or discouraged,
for the LORD will personally go ahead of you."

DEUT. 31:8

Those who live in the shelter of the Most High will find rest
in the shadow of the Almighty.

Ps. 91:1

"I will never fail you. I will never abandon you."

Heb. 13:5

Kind words are like honey – sweet to the soul and healthy for the body.

Prov. 16:24

"The joy of the LORD is your strength!"

NEH. 8:10

This is the day the LORD has made.
We will rejoice and be glad in it.

Ps. 118:24

Those who trust in the LORD will find new strength.
They will soar high on wings like eagles.

ISA. 40:31

"No eye has seen, no ear has heard, and no mind has imagined what God has prepared for those who love Him."

1 Cor. 2:9

I will rejoice in the LORD! I will be joyful in the God of my salvation!

HAB. 3:18

Nothing in all creation will ever be able to separate us from the love of God.

Rom. 8:39

My health may fail, and my spirit may grow weak, but God remains the strength of my heart; He is mine forever.

Ps. 73:26

See how very much our Father loves us, for He calls us
His children, and that is what we are!

1 John 3:1

"Blessed are all who hear the word of God
and put it into practice."

Luke 11:28

The Lord is my light and my salvation –
so why should I be afraid?

Ps. 27:1

The Lord is my strength and my song; He has given me victory.
This is my God, and I will praise Him.

Exod. 15:2

May the Lord of peace Himself give you His peace
at all times and in every situation.

2 Thess. 3:16

Let the peace that comes from Christ rule in your hearts.
For as members of one body you are called to live in peace.

Col. 3:15

LORD my God, I cried to You for help, and You restored my health.

Ps. 30:2

"Those who exalt themselves will be humbled,
and those who humble themselves will be exalted."

Matt. 23:12

"Do not be afraid, for I have ransomed you. I have called you by name; you are Mine. When you go through deep waters, I will be with you."

Isa. 43:1-2

"Be still, and know that I am God!"

Ps. 46:10

"I know the plans I have for you," says the LORD. "They are plans for good and not for disaster, to give you a future and a hope."

JER. 29:11

"Be strong and courageous!
For the LORD your God is with you wherever you go."

JOSH. 1:9

He made us, and we are His. We are His people, the sheep of His pasture.

Ps. 100:3

Give your burdens to the LORD, and He will take care of you.

Ps. 55:22

Let God transform you into a new person by changing the way you think.

Rom. 12:2

"God blesses those who work for peace,
for they will be called the children of God."

Matt. 5:9

"Anything is possible if a person believes."

MARK 9:23

I can do everything through Christ, who gives me strength.

Phil. 4:13

"Blessed are those who trust in the LORD and have made the LORD their hope and confidence."

JER. 17:7

The Lord leads with unfailing love and faithfulness
all who keep His covenant and obey His demands.

Ps. 25:10

"Come to Me, all of you who are weary and carry heavy burdens,
and I will give you rest."

Matt. 11:28

"Do not be afraid or discouraged,
for the LORD will personally go ahead of you."

DEUT. 31:8

Those who live in the shelter of the Most High will find rest
in the shadow of the Almighty.

Ps. 91:1

"I will never fail you. I will never abandon you."

Heb. 13:5

Kind words are like honey – sweet to the soul and healthy for the body.

Prov. 16:24

"The joy of the Lord is your strength!"

Neh. 8:10

This is the day the LORD has made.
We will rejoice and be glad in it.

Ps. 118:24

Those who trust in the LORD will find new strength.
They will soar high on wings like eagles.

ISA. 40:31

"No eye has seen, no ear has heard, and no mind has imagined what God has prepared for those who love Him."

1 Cor. 2:9

I will rejoice in the LORD! I will be joyful in the God of my salvation!

HAB. 3:18

Nothing in all creation will ever be able to separate us from the love of God.

Rom. 8:39

My health may fail, and my spirit may grow weak, but God remains the strength of my heart; He is mine forever.

Ps. 73:26

See how very much our Father loves us, for He calls us
His children, and that is what we are!

1 John 3:1

"Blessed are all who hear the word of God
and put it into practice."

LUKE 11:28

The LORD is my light and my salvation –
so why should I be afraid?

Ps. 27:1

The LORD is my strength and my song; He has given me victory.
This is my God, and I will praise Him.

EXOD. 15:2

May the Lord of peace Himself give you His peace
at all times and in every situation.

2 Thess. 3:16

Let the peace that comes from Christ rule in your hearts.
For as members of one body you are called to live in peace.

Col. 3:15

Lord my God, I cried to You for help, and You restored my health.

Ps. 30:2

"Those who exalt themselves will be humbled,
and those who humble themselves will be exalted."

MATT. 23:12

"Do not be afraid, for I have ransomed you. I have called you by name; you are Mine. When you go through deep waters, I will be with you."

Isa. 43:1-2

"Be still, and know that I am God!"

Ps. 46:10

"I know the plans I have for you," says the LORD. "They are plans for good and not for disaster, to give you a future and a hope."

JER. 29:11

"Be strong and courageous!
For the LORD your God is with you wherever you go."

JOSH. 1:9

He made us, and we are His. We are His people, the sheep of His pasture.

Ps. 100:3

Give your burdens to the LORD, and He will take care of you.

PS. 55:22

Let God transform you into a new person by changing the way you think.

Rom. 12:2

"God blesses those who work for peace,
for they will be called the children of God."

MATT. 5:9

"Anything is possible if a person believes."

MARK 9:23

I can do everything through Christ, who gives me strength.

PHIL. 4:13

"Blessed are those who trust in the LORD and have made the LORD their hope and confidence."

JER. 17:7

The LORD leads with unfailing love and faithfulness
all who keep His covenant and obey His demands.

Ps. 25:10

"Come to Me, all of you who are weary and carry heavy burdens,
and I will give you rest."

Matt. 11:28

"Do not be afraid or discouraged,
for the LORD will personally go ahead of you."

DEUT. 31:8

Those who live in the shelter of the Most High will find rest
in the shadow of the Almighty.

Ps. 91:1

"I will never fail you. I will never abandon you."

Heb. 13:5

Kind words are like honey – sweet to the soul and healthy for the body.

Prov. 16:24

"The joy of the LORD is your strength!"

NEH. 8:10

This is the day the LORD has made.
We will rejoice and be glad in it.

Ps. 118:24

Those who trust in the LORD will find new strength.
They will soar high on wings like eagles.

ISA. 40:31

"No eye has seen, no ear has heard, and no mind has imagined what God has prepared for those who love Him."

1 Cor. 2:9

I will rejoice in the LORD! I will be joyful in the God of my salvation!

HAB. 3:18

Nothing in all creation will ever be able to separate us from the love of God.

Rom. 8:39

My health may fail, and my spirit may grow weak, but God remains the strength of my heart; He is mine forever.

Ps. 73:26

See how very much our Father loves us, for He calls us
His children, and that is what we are!

1 John 3:1

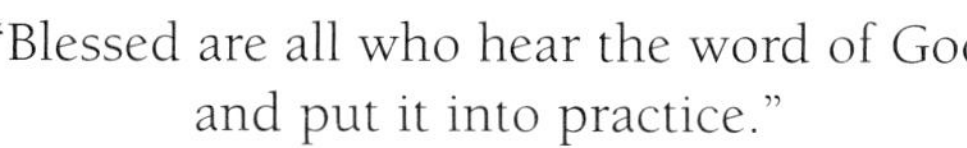

"Blessed are all who hear the word of God
and put it into practice."

Luke 11:28

The LORD is my light and my salvation –
so why should I be afraid?

Ps. 27:1

The LORD is my strength and my song; He has given me victory.
This is my God, and I will praise Him.

EXOD. 15:2

May the Lord of peace Himself give you His peace
at all times and in every situation.

2 Thess. 3:16

Let the peace that comes from Christ rule in your hearts.
For as members of one body you are called to live in peace.

Col. 3:15

Lord my God, I cried to You for help, and You restored my health.

Ps. 30:2

"Those who exalt themselves will be humbled,
and those who humble themselves will be exalted."

Matt. 23:12

"Do not be afraid, for I have ransomed you. I have called you by name; you are Mine. When you go through deep waters, I will be with you."

Isa. 43:1-2

"Be still, and know that I am God!"

Ps. 46:10

"I know the plans I have for you," says the Lord. "They are plans for good and not for disaster, to give you a future and a hope."

Jer. 29:11

"Be strong and courageous!
For the LORD your God is with you wherever you go."

JOSH. 1:9

He made us, and we are His. We are His people, the sheep of His pasture.

Ps. 100:3

Give your burdens to the LORD, and He will take care of you.

Ps. 55:22

Let God transform you into a new person by changing the way you think.

Rom. 12:2

"God blesses those who work for peace,
for they will be called the children of God."

MATT. 5:9

"Anything is possible if a person believes."

Mark 9:23

I can do everything through Christ, who gives me strength.

PHIL. 4:13

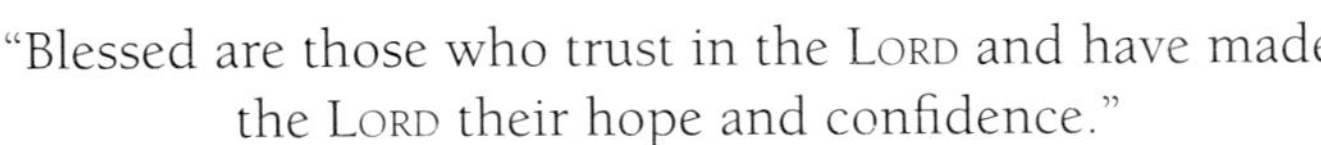

"Blessed are those who trust in the Lord and have made the Lord their hope and confidence."

Jer. 17:7

The Lord leads with unfailing love and faithfulness
all who keep His covenant and obey His demands.

Ps. 25:10

"Come to Me, all of you who are weary and carry heavy burdens, and I will give you rest."

Matt. 11:28

"Do not be afraid or discouraged,
for the Lord will personally go ahead of you."

Deut. 31:8

Those who live in the shelter of the Most High will find rest
in the shadow of the Almighty.

Ps. 91:1

"I will never fail you. I will never abandon you."

Heb. 13:5

Kind words are like honey – sweet to the soul and healthy for the body.

Prov. 16:24

"The joy of the LORD is your strength!"

NEH. 8:10

This is the day the LORD has made.
We will rejoice and be glad in it.

Ps. 118:24

Those who trust in the LORD will find new strength.
They will soar high on wings like eagles.

ISA. 40:31

"No eye has seen, no ear has heard, and no mind has imagined what God has prepared for those who love Him."

1 Cor. 2:9

I will rejoice in the LORD! I will be joyful in the God of my salvation!

HAB. 3:18

Nothing in all creation will ever be able to separate us from the love of God.

Rom. 8:39

My health may fail, and my spirit may grow weak, but God remains the strength of my heart; He is mine forever.

Ps. 73:26

See how very much our Father loves us, for He calls us His children, and that is what we are!

1 John 3:1

"Blessed are all who hear the word of God
and put it into practice."

Luke 11:28

The LORD is my light and my salvation –
so why should I be afraid?

Ps. 27:1

The LORD is my strength and my song; He has given me victory.
This is my God, and I will praise Him.

EXOD. 15:2

May the Lord of peace Himself give you His peace
at all times and in every situation.

2 Thess. 3:16

Let the peace that comes from Christ rule in your hearts.
For as members of one body you are called to live in peace.

Col. 3:15

LORD my God, I cried to You for help, and You restored my health.

Ps. 30:2

"Those who exalt themselves will be humbled,
and those who humble themselves will be exalted."

MATT. 23:12

"Do not be afraid, for I have ransomed you. I have called you by name; you are Mine. When you go through deep waters, I will be with you."

Isa. 43:1-2

"Be still, and know that I am God!"

Ps. 46:10

"I know the plans I have for you," says the LORD. "They are plans for good and not for disaster, to give you a future and a hope."

JER. 29:11

"Be strong and courageous!
For the LORD your God is with you wherever you go."

JOSH. 1:9

He made us, and we are His. We are His people, the sheep of His pasture.

Ps. 100:3

Give your burdens to the LORD, and He will take care of you.

PS. 55:22

Let God transform you into a new person by changing the way you think.

Rom. 12:2

"God blesses those who work for peace,
for they will be called the children of God."

Matt. 5:9

"Anything is possible if a person believes."

Mark 9:23

I can do everything through Christ, who gives me strength.

Phil. 4:13

"Blessed are those who trust in the LORD and have made the LORD their hope and confidence."

JER. 17:7

The LORD leads with unfailing love and faithfulness
all who keep His covenant and obey His demands.

Ps. 25:10

"Come to Me, all of you who are weary and carry heavy burdens, and I will give you rest."

Matt. 11:28

"Do not be afraid or discouraged,
for the LORD will personally go ahead of you."

DEUT. 31:8

Those who live in the shelter of the Most High will find rest
in the shadow of the Almighty.

Ps. 91:1

"I will never fail you. I will never abandon you."

Heb. 13:5

Kind words are like honey – sweet to the soul and healthy for the body.

Prov. 16:24

"The joy of the Lord is your strength!"

Neh. 8:10

This is the day the LORD has made.
We will rejoice and be glad in it.

Ps. 118:24

Those who trust in the LORD will find new strength.
They will soar high on wings like eagles.

ISA. 40:31

"No eye has seen, no ear has heard, and no mind has imagined what God has prepared for those who love Him."

1 Cor. 2:9

I will rejoice in the LORD! I will be joyful in the God of my salvation!

HAB. 3:18

Nothing in all creation will ever be able to separate us from the love of God.

Rom. 8:39

My health may fail, and my spirit may grow weak, but God remains the strength of my heart; He is mine forever.

Ps. 73:26

See how very much our Father loves us, for He calls us
His children, and that is what we are!

1 John 3:1

"Blessed are all who hear the word of God
and put it into practice."

LUKE 11:28

The LORD is my light and my salvation –
so why should I be afraid?

Ps. 27:1

The LORD is my strength and my song; He has given me victory.
This is my God, and I will praise Him.

EXOD. 15:2

May the Lord of peace Himself give you His peace
at all times and in every situation.

2 Thess. 3:16

Let the peace that comes from Christ rule in your hearts.
For as members of one body you are called to live in peace.

Col. 3:15

LORD my God, I cried to You for help, and You restored my health.

Ps. 30:2

"Those who exalt themselves will be humbled,
and those who humble themselves will be exalted."

MATT. 23:12

“Do not be afraid, for I have ransomed you. I have called you by name; you are Mine. When you go through deep waters, I will be with you.”

Isa. 43:1-2

"Be still, and know that I am God!"

Ps. 46:10

"I know the plans I have for you," says the LORD. "They are plans for good and not for disaster, to give you a future and a hope."

JER. 29:11

"Be strong and courageous!
For the LORD your God is with you wherever you go."

JOSH. 1:9

He made us, and we are His. We are His people, the sheep of His pasture.

Ps. 100:3

Give your burdens to the LORD, and He will take care of you.

PS. 55:22

Let God transform you into a new person by changing the way you think.

Rom. 12:2

"God blesses those who work for peace,
for they will be called the children of God."

MATT. 5:9

"Anything is possible if a person believes."

Mark 9:23

I can do everything through Christ, who gives me strength.

PHIL. 4:13

"Blessed are those who trust in the LORD and have made the LORD their hope and confidence."

JER. 17:7

The LORD leads with unfailing love and faithfulness
all who keep His covenant and obey His demands.

PS. 25:10

"Come to Me, all of you who are weary and carry heavy burdens, and I will give you rest."

Matt. 11:28

"Do not be afraid or discouraged,
for the LORD will personally go ahead of you."

DEUT. 31:8

Those who live in the shelter of the Most High will find rest
in the shadow of the Almighty.

Ps. 91:1

"I will never fail you. I will never abandon you."

HEB. 13:5

Kind words are like honey – sweet to the soul and healthy for the body.

Prov. 16:24

"The joy of the LORD is your strength!"

NEH. 8:10

This is the day the LORD has made.
We will rejoice and be glad in it.

Ps. 118:24

Those who trust in the LORD will find new strength.
They will soar high on wings like eagles.

ISA. 40:31

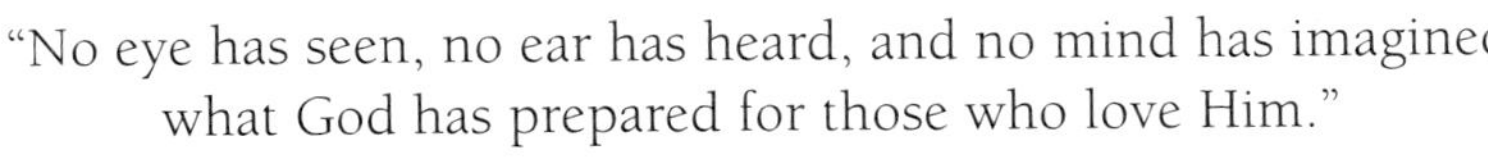

"No eye has seen, no ear has heard, and no mind has imagined what God has prepared for those who love Him."

1 Cor. 2:9

I will rejoice in the LORD! I will be joyful in the God of my salvation!

HAB. 3:18

Nothing in all creation will ever be able to separate us from the love of God.

Rom. 8:39

My health may fail, and my spirit may grow weak, but God remains the strength of my heart; He is mine forever.

Ps. 73:26

See how very much our Father loves us, for He calls us
His children, and that is what we are!

1 John 3:1

"Blessed are all who hear the word of God
and put it into practice."

Luke 11:28

The LORD is my light and my salvation –
so why should I be afraid?

Ps. 27:1

The LORD is my strength and my song; He has given me victory.
This is my God, and I will praise Him.

EXOD. 15:2

May the Lord of peace Himself give you His peace
at all times and in every situation.

2 Thess. 3:16

Let the peace that comes from Christ rule in your hearts.
For as members of one body you are called to live in peace.

Col. 3:15

LORD my God, I cried to You for help, and You restored my health.

Ps. 30:2

“Those who exalt themselves will be humbled,
and those who humble themselves will be exalted.”

Matt. 23:12

"Do not be afraid, for I have ransomed you. I have called you by name; you are Mine. When you go through deep waters, I will be with you."

Isa. 43:1-2

"Be still, and know that I am God!"

Ps. 46:10

"I know the plans I have for you," says the LORD. "They are plans for good and not for disaster, to give you a future and a hope."

JER. 29:11

"Be strong and courageous!
For the LORD your God is with you wherever you go."

JOSH. 1:9

He made us, and we are His. We are His people, the sheep of His pasture.

Ps. 100:3

Give your burdens to the LORD, and He will take care of you.

Ps. 55:22

Let God transform you into a new person by changing the way you think.

Rom. 12:2

"God blesses those who work for peace,
for they will be called the children of God."

Matt. 5:9

"Anything is possible if a person believes."

Mark 9:23

I can do everything through Christ, who gives me strength.

PHIL. 4:13

"Blessed are those who trust in the LORD and have made the LORD their hope and confidence."

JER. 17:7

The LORD leads with unfailing love and faithfulness
all who keep His covenant and obey His demands.

Ps. 25:10

"Come to Me, all of you who are weary and carry heavy burdens, and I will give you rest."

MATT. 11:28

"Do not be afraid or discouraged,
for the LORD will personally go ahead of you."

DEUT. 31:8

Those who live in the shelter of the Most High will find rest
in the shadow of the Almighty.

Ps. 91:1

"I will never fail you. I will never abandon you."

Heb. 13:5

Kind words are like honey – sweet to the soul and healthy for the body.

Prov. 16:24